KU-053-499

START-UP SCIENCE

Loud and Quiet

By Jack Challoner

Contents

Belitha Press

ROTHERHAM LIBRARY &
INFORMATION SERVICES

JS34
809 208 9
R00003481
SCHOOLS STOCK

First published in Great Britain in 1996 by
 Belitha Press Ltd, London House,
Great Eastern Wharf, Parkgate Road,
London SW11 4NQ

Copyright © in this format Belitha Press Ltd 1996
Text © Jack Challoner 1996

All rights reserved. No part of this book may be reproduced
or utilized in any form or by any means, electronic or
mechanical, including photocopying, recording or by any
information storage or retrieval system without permission
from the publisher except by a reviewer who
may quote brief passages in a review.

British Library Cataloguing in
Publication Data for this book
is available from the British Library.

Acknowledgements

Bubbles: 20 Ian West.
Bruce Coleman: 21 bottom Chris James.
FLPA: 11 centre Martin Withers, 13 top D P Wilson,
17 centre and 31 E & D Hosking, 18 P Berry, 19 A Wharton.
NHPA: 27 Stephen Dalton.
Oxford Scientific Films: 8 John Downer, 29 Tony Martin, 30 Eyal Bartov.
Planet Earth Pictures: 10 and 12 John Lythgoe,
13 centre G Van Ryckevorsel.
Science Photo Library: 9 top Keith Kent,
11 top Martin Bond, 26 Dr Morley Read,
28 Sinclair Stammers.

All other photographs by Claire Paxton
Thanks to models Harry, Alex, Sally, Donisha, Samantha,
Ruman, Hayley, Leila, Poonam, Jack, Himansu, Peter, Andy, Hardik

ISBN 1-85561-508-8

Edited by Liz Harman
Series design by Hayley Cove
Designed by Helen James
Illustrated by David Gifford
Picture research by Juliet Duff and Diana Morris

Science adviser Geoff Leyland,
Head Teacher, Hady Primary School,
Chesterfield

Printed in Spain

Words in **bold** appear in the glossary on page 32.

Loud and quiet

This book will answer lots of questions that you may have about loud and quiet things. But it will also make you think for yourself.

Each time you turn a page, you will find an activity that you can do yourself at home or at school. You may need help from an adult.

When there are lots of loud sounds around you, it is noisy. What makes some sounds louder than others?

Loud sounds

The more noise something makes, the louder it is. You can hear loud sounds from a long way away. Noisy things sound louder the closer you are to them.

Did you know?

One of the loudest sounds ever heard in the world was caused by a volcano called Krakatoa. The sound of Krakatoa **erupting** in 1883 could be heard thousands of kilometres away.

Noisy fireworks

The whizzes and bangs of a fireworks display can be heard from far away. The fireworks make lots of noise as they explode high in the air.

Take-off

Aeroplanes can be very noisy when they take off. The nearer you are to them, the louder they sound.

Now try this

You can hear a loud sound when you hit a spoon against a table.

You will need
A metal spoon, some string.

1 Tie the string to the handle of the spoon.

2 Wrap one end of the string around a finger and press the finger against one ear.

3 Now dangle the spoon from the string, and tap it against the side of a table. You should hear some loud sounds.

Quiet things

Things that do not make much noise are quiet. We need to be very close to quiet things and to listen carefully in order to hear them properly.

Did you know?

Owls have very good hearing. This helps them to find small animals, such as mice, when they are hunting at night.

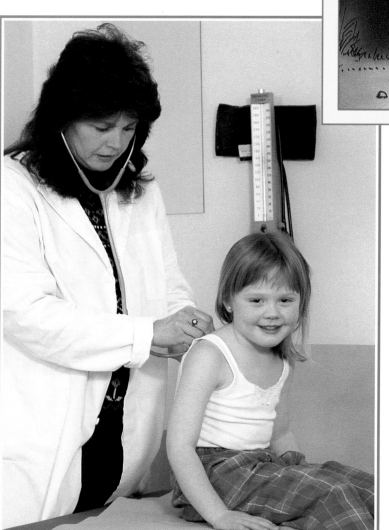

Beating heart

Can you hear your heart beating? This doctor is using an instrument called a **stethoscope**, which makes the girl's quiet heartbeat sound much louder.

Listening quietly

Sometimes you need to be quiet. When someone reads a story, you will not be able to hear unless you listen quietly.

Now try this

You can see for yourself how a stethoscope can help you to hear quiet sounds.

You will need
A cardboard tube, a watch that ticks.

1 Hold one end of the tube gently against your ear.

2 Now put the other end of the tube over the watch. Can you hear the watch ticking?

Making sound

The more sound something makes, the louder it is. Objects must move backwards and forwards very quickly, or **vibrate**, to make sound.

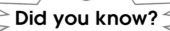

Did you know?

There are two flaps in your throat, called **vocal cords**. They vibrate when air passes over them as you speak or sing.

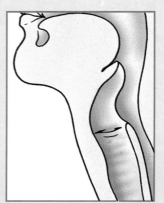

Noisy balloon

A balloon can make a sound when you stretch its neck. The rubber at the neck of the balloon vibrates as air escapes from the balloon.

Paper cone

This **loudspeaker** makes sound when the **hi-fi** is switched on. Inside the loudspeaker is a paper cone that vibrates and makes the sound.

Now try this

You can feel the vibrations of a loudspeaker by using a balloon.

You will need
A balloon, a balloon pump, a hi-fi or portable cassette player.

1 Blow up the balloon using the pump. Ask an adult to tie the neck of the balloon.

2 Ask an adult to turn on the hi-fi. Hold the balloon between one loudspeaker and your ear.

3 Ask an adult to make the hi-fi louder. Does the balloon vibrate more or less?

Travelling sound

An object that vibrates makes sound. The sound travels through the air from the object so that we can hear it. Sounds can also travel through solid objects.

Blowing a whistle

Can you see the man blowing his whistle? The sound the whistle makes travels through the air in all directions, so that the children can hear it.

Did you know?

The fastest cars in the world have rockets to push them along at great speed. But even the fastest cars cannot travel as fast as sound.

Travelling through wood

This girl is making the table vibrate by tapping it with a pencil. The vibrations travel through the table, and the boy can hear the sound.

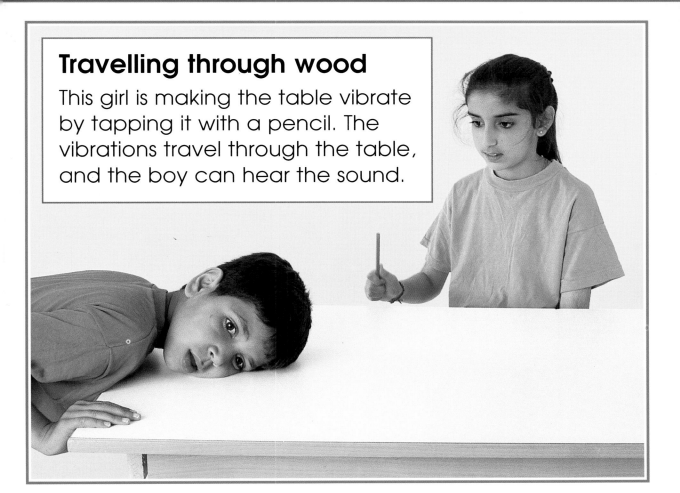

Now try this

Sound travels through the air quite quickly. But sometimes you can see something happen before you hear the sound.

1 With an adult and a friend go into a park or the school grounds.

2 Ask your friend to walk about 100 metres away from you and to clap. You should see the hands clapping before you hear the sound.

Sound waves

Any object that vibrates disturbs the air around it. The sound it makes travels in all directions, as invisible **sound waves**, so that people nearby can hear it.

Seeing sound waves

Did you know?

The sound waves of a high sound, like a whistle, are closer together than those of a low sound, like a tuba.

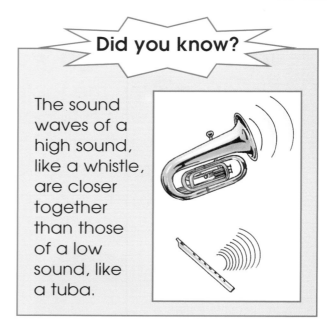

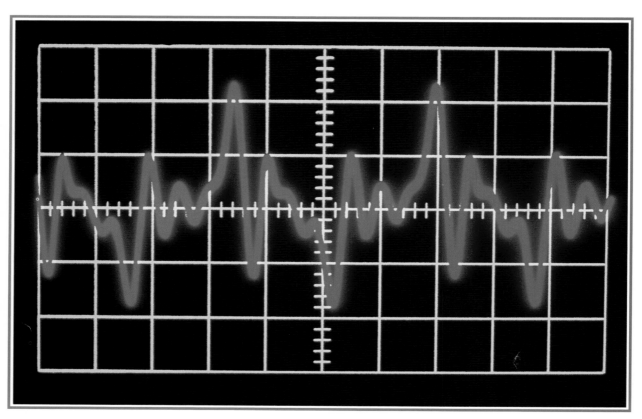

This picture shows sound waves made by someone speaking. A special machine called an **oscilloscope** shows the sound waves on a screen.

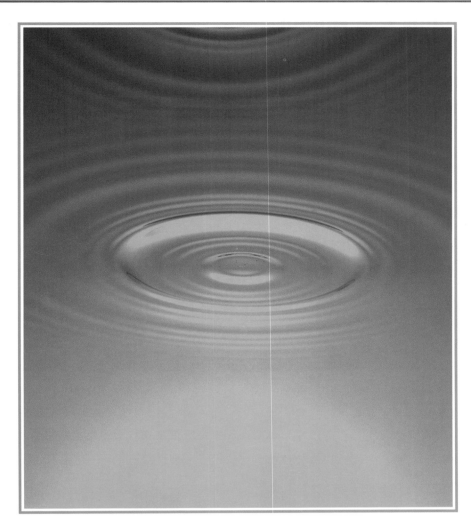

Water waves

When you drop something into water, it disturbs the water and makes waves. The waves travel out in all directions, just like sound waves.

Now try this

You can see for yourself how water waves are made.

You will need
A bowl filled with water.

1 Roll up your sleeves and hold one finger just above the water.

2 Touch the surface of the water and move your finger gently up and down. You should see waves moving outwards.

Bouncing sound

Sometimes a sound travelling through the air will bounce off a hard object, such as a wall. A sound that has bounced off something is called an **echo**.

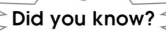

Did you know?

Some ships bounce sound off the bottom of the sea, so that they can tell how deep the sea is. If the echo returns very soon, the sea is shallow.

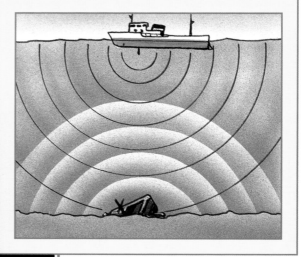

Hearing echoes

This woman is calling to her friend, who has walked into a tunnel. The sound of her voice bounces off the hard stone and comes back as an echo.

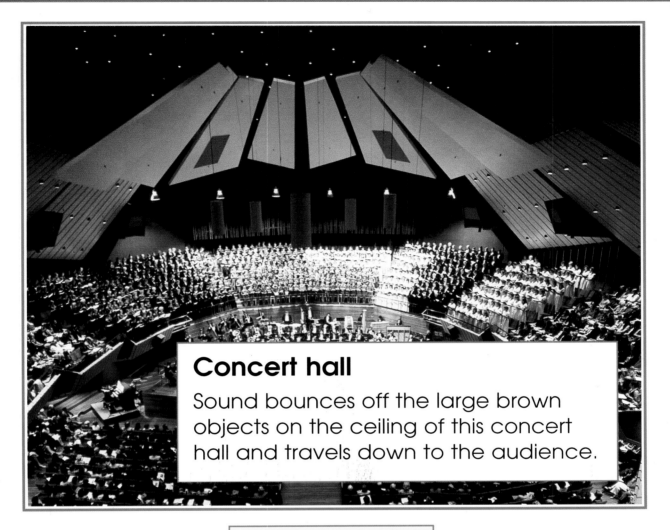

Concert hall

Sound bounces off the large brown objects on the ceiling of this concert hall and travels down to the audience.

Now try this

Sound only bounces off hard objects, such as walls. It will not bounce off soft objects, such as curtains.

1 Stand in a bathroom, or a large hallway and clap your hands. Listen carefully for an echo.

2 Try clapping your hands in other rooms. Rooms with curtains, chairs or beds will not make echoes.

How we hear

We hear sounds with our ears and our brains. Most people can hear loud sounds and quiet sounds. But how do our ears work?

Did you know?

People who are hard of hearing cannot hear sounds very well. Long ago, people who were hard of hearing used ear trumpets like this.

Ear drum

Inside our ears is a piece of skin called the **ear drum**. As sound hits it, it vibrates, sending messages to our brain, so we hear the sound.

Hearing aid

This is a hearing aid. A tiny **microphone** inside picks up sounds, and the hearing aid makes them louder. This helps the man to hear sound better.

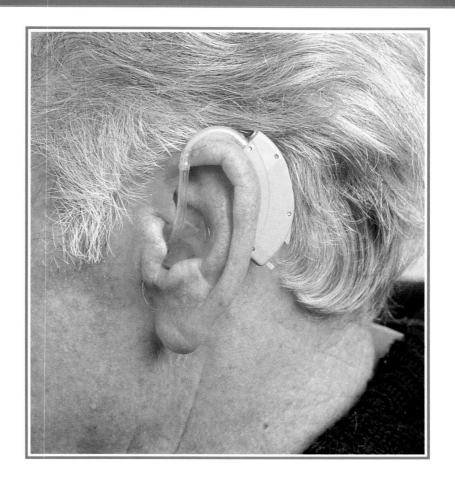

Now try this

You can see how ear drums vibrate as sound hits them.

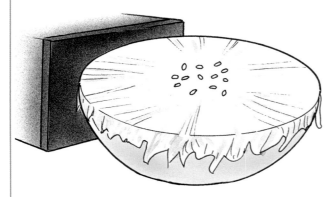

You will need
A glass bowl, plastic food wrap, uncooked rice grains, a hi-fi or portable cassette player.

1 Ask an adult to stretch the plastic food wrap over the bowl.

2 Place a few rice grains on top of the bowl and put it next to the loudspeaker of the hi-fi.

3 Turn on the music quite loud. You should see the rice grains bounce up and down.

Animal ears

There are almost as many types of animal ears as there are different types of animal. Many animals' ears are shaped so that they catch lots of sound.

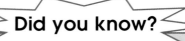

Did you know?

A crocodile's ears are just behind its eyes. The ears have flaps of skin which close to keep the water out.

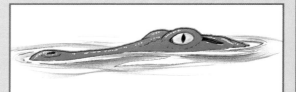

Big ears

This hare has very large ears. It can hear very well because more sound travels into its large ears than it would into smaller ears.

No ears?

This insect is a cricket. It has no ears on its head. It hears sound with tiny ears on its legs.

Now try this

A hare's large ears mean that it can hear very well. You can see for yourself how this works using a radio.

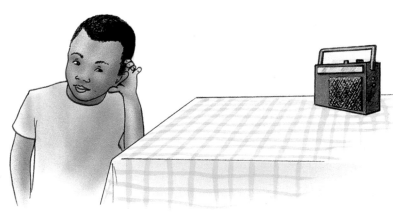

You will need
A radio.

1 Turn on the radio very quietly, so that you can just hear it.

2 Sit near the radio, and cup one hand behind your ear.

3 Listen carefully. You should be able to hear the radio better.

High and low sounds

If an object vibrates very quickly, it will make a high sound, like a whistle. If it vibrates slowly, it will make a low sound, like a drum.

Did you know?

Whistles make high sounds. A dog whistle makes a sound that is too high for humans to hear, but which dogs can hear.

Big drum

As the drummer hits the skin of this big drum, the skin vibrates quite slowly. This makes a very low sound. A bigger drum might make a sound that is too low to be heard.

High notes

This opera singer can sing very high notes. When we sing high notes, our vocal cords stretch, so that they can vibrate more quickly.

Now try this

When you sing a high note, your vocal cords stretch. You can feel this for yourself.

1 Hold your throat gently between a finger and thumb.

2 Sing a low note. Can you feel your throat vibrating?

3 Now sing a high note. You should feel your throat stretching.

Music from strings

Some musical instruments make sounds using strings. Strings held tightly at each end vibrate when they are plucked with a finger or rubbed with a bow.

Long and short

This harp player makes sounds by plucking the harp strings. The short strings make high notes, and the longer strings make lower notes.

Did you know?

A piano contains many strings. When a key is pressed, a hammer strikes a string inside and plays a note.

Using a bow

The strings of this violin vibrate as the man moves the bow across them. The man changes the note by pressing his fingers on the strings.

Now try this

You can see for yourself how shorter strings make higher notes.

You will need
A shoe box, a rubber band, a pencil.

1 Stretch the rubber band over the box, and push the pencil under the rubber band.

2 Now pluck the rubber band. Move the pencil so that you pluck a shorter piece of the

rubber band. Is the note higher or lower than before?

Music from air

Air in a pipe can be made to vibrate. When it does, it makes sound. The sound is higher in a short pipe than in a long one.

Did you know?

Covering all the holes on a recorder with your fingers makes a low note. This is because covering all the holes makes the recorder into a long pipe.

Air in pipes

These organ pipes can make loud sounds, as air vibrates inside them. The long pipes make low sounds, and the short pipes make higher sounds.

Mouth music

These trombone players blow through their lips to make the air inside their trombones vibrate. Making the tube longer or shorter changes the note.

Now try this

You can make your own musical sound from air. Different amounts of air make different notes.

You will need
A clean plastic bottle, water.

1 Put some water into the bottle.

2 Put your bottom lip against the neck of the bottle, and blow gently. You should hear a sound.

3 Add more water. Does the note become higher or lower?

Animal noises

Most animals make some sort of sound. Usually the sound sends a message to other animals. This is called **communication**.

Did you know?

Whales use loud sounds to communicate with each other. They can be heard hundreds of kilometres away.

Noisy snake

Dried skin in this rattlesnake's tail makes a rattling sound as the tail moves. The sound frightens away animals that might attack the snake.

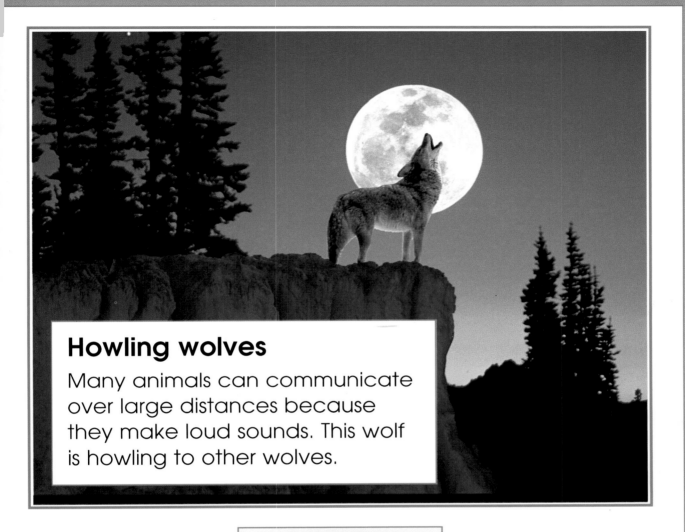

Howling wolves

Many animals can communicate over large distances because they make loud sounds. This wolf is howling to other wolves.

Now try this

You can see for yourself how rattlesnakes make a rattling sound.

You will need
Uncooked rice grains or dried beans, an empty one litre plastic bottle.

1 Put a handful of rice or beans in the bottle.

2 Screw on the lid of the bottle.

3 Shake the bottle and you will hear a rattling sound. It will be louder the harder you shake.

Loud and quiet places

In places where there is a lot happening, such as a factory, it is noisy. Some places are so noisy you could hurt your ears if you stayed there for too long.

Did you know?

In space there is no sound, because there is no air for it to travel through. Astronauts in space communicate with each other using radios.

Looking after our ears

People who work with noisy machines often have to wear **ear defenders** to protect their ears. These stop much of the sound from entering their ears.

Quiet room

This recording studio is a very quiet place. The walls of the studio are very thick and the door is shut tight. No sound comes in.

Now try this

You can see for yourself how ear defenders work.

You will need
Two polystyrene cups, a clean pair of socks, a radio.

1 Push one sock into each cup.

2 Turn on the radio.

3 Hold one cup firmly over each of your ears. Can you still hear?

Recorded sound

When you play a compact disc or a cassette, you may hear sounds that were made a long time ago. The sounds were recorded using microphones.

Did you know?

The first machine ever to record sound was called a **phonograph**.

Not too loud

Our ears are very sensitive. Too much loud noise can harm them. If you use a personal stereo, you should not play it too loudly.

Using a microphone

Inside this microphone is a part called a **diaphragm**, which works like an ear drum. As sound hits the diaphragm, it vibrates. Microphones can be used to record sound.

Now try this

Can you tell what something is just by the sound it makes? Record some different sounds, and see if your friends can guess what they are.

You will need
A cassette recorder with a microphone, a blank cassette, some objects that will make noises.

1 Ask an adult to help you to set up the cassette recorder, and to record some sounds.

2 Play back the sounds to your friends and see if they can guess what made the sounds.

Glossary

communicate To talk or send messages.

diaphragm A vibrating disc inside a telephone, microphone or loudspeaker.

ear defenders Special pads worn over the ears to protect them from very loud noises.

ear drum A delicate skin stretched across the inside of the ear.

echo A sound that has bounced off a hard surface.

erupting Exploding.

hi-fi A machine used to listen to radio, cassettes, records or compact discs.

loudspeaker An object that uses electricity to make sounds.

microphone A device that makes sound into electricity.

oscilloscope A machine that allows sound waves to be shown on a computer screen.

phonograph An early type of record-player

sound waves The way that sound travels through the air.

stethoscope An instrument used to listen to the heart or lungs.

vibrate To move very rapidly to and fro.

vocal cords The part of the human body that produces the voice.

Index